Prayers to Stay the Course of Marriage

Queen Elizabeth Gardner

Cover designed by Tammie T. Polk

Queen E. Gardner
Find me online at www.amazon.com

Printed in the United States of America

First Printing: May 2021
Amazon/KDP

ISBN-13   978-0-578-92248-5

Thanks to my mother and father for teaching me to pray through whatever storms that comes into my life and teaching me that nothing is impossible with God on my side, to Minister Eugenia Sims and her husband Carlos Sims for introduction my husband and me at a time when we both needed someone to comfort us, to my Pastor and his wife, Dr. Harry and Lady Beverly Davis, for always lending a listening ear whenever I need to talk and pray, to my family always being supportive and praying with me whenever I needed them.

A special thanks to my husband for encouraging me to publish this book so others can share in our road to a successful marriage.

In everything give thanks: for this is the will of God in Christ Jesus concerning you.

—I THESSALONIANS 5:18

Foreward by Tamara Flemings

What inspirational words can be said about a woman that has inspired so many?

Queen Gardner is first and foremost a woman of God. She has dedicated her life to spreading the word of God to His flock. She inspires people to be the best of themselves with a simple conversation. She presents herself approved to God as a worker who does not need to be ashamed, handling accurately the word of truth.

Queen is family orientated, strong and loving. Family comes first, second only to God. She is loved in return by her family and friends. Friends that are like family. She is giving of herself to help others in need. Her heart is filled with love that could cover the universe and it is apparent when she enters a room.

Queen is a fitting name for this woman of God, wife, mother, sibling, aunt, and friend.

Preface

Marriage is a marathon, not a sprint. No matter how strong a marriage is there are still challenges. Those challenges could be financial, physical, mental, spiritual, emotional, or any number of issues. However, prayer is the answer to all our problems.

If spouses would pray, in faith, for one another, God will lead and guide them to a place of peace and harmony. When we learn to encourage one another and find the good in every situation, instead of finding faults, criticizing or insulting each other, we will also learn to respect each other's perspectives. As we learn to lift each other up in prayer before the Lord, we began to work better together.

Prayer is so powerful; it works in a way that is unexplainable. Before you know it, all the wheels of marriage are turning so smooth that it seems there was never a glitch in the first place.

Introduction

When my husband and I first met, it was at a pivotal time in his life. He had recently lost his wife. He was grieving the loss of his wife and learning to handle all the many chores of the home and handling the everyday business along with suffering an illness of his own. He was working three part-time jobs and going through alcoholism due to the pains of things that had gone on in his life and pain caused by "gout."

I had lost my husband a few years earlier and had gone through many of the same struggles but had gotten through the rough stages and was well on way to a life of comfort.

I am one of the two female ministers at the church I attend. My husband is friends to the other minister's husband. He suggested we meet and talk, since we both had similar circumstances and it seemed I was doing well. I thought I was just meeting him to help him through his grieving period, at least that was the plan. However, during the time spent with him I recognized an incredibly unique and humble man, so I fell in love with him. We started dating but he was not ready for a serious relationship. After six years of dating, I thought marriage should be the next step for our relationship, but he had reservations because he only had a part-time job and concerned about being able to support a family. Remember I told you there would be challenges.

After convincing him that God will make a way for us if we do the right thing, he proposed, and we were married.

Thus, prayer and a whole lot of encouragement was the key to our successful marriage. We had a hard time understanding each other's way of thinking and communicating. We were raised differently, and our values were not the same, the only things we had in common was our love for God and each other. However, our faith foundation was the same. We both believed in Jesus Chris as our Lord and Savior and the Holy Bible is the true word of God. As we struggled to communicate and come together as one in the Lord, I would write prayers and leave them on the table, by the coffee pot, on his bathroom mirror or in his lunch bag. The one thing we did agree on was that prayer is the key and faith unlocks doors. Pray is truly what kept us in peace until we could merge as one.

We have been married for seven years now and although there are still challenges, he is now employed full-time and through prayer we are running this marathon of marriage together.

Our faith in Christ Jesus is our foundation and we keep Him at the head and center of our marriage everyday of our lives.

This book is a book of daily prayers and encouragements to my husband who is now employed full-time and taking care of his family in ways he never thought possible.

It is my prayer that this book can help other couples find their way in a dark world where it seems there is no way out. The family that prays together, stay together.

Cold Weather Blessings

Good morning, My Darling Husband!
Please dress warm today.
We both have a long day,
I miss you already.
Please know I love, love, love you.

My Prayer for You

Dear Father God,
Thank you for Your Grace & Mercy.
You have opened so many doors for us.
You have given my husband favor at work so he can work more
hours and even allowed him to have an extra job.
Lord, for that we are so thankful.
Now Lord, please keep him safe and healthy.
Protect us while we are apart and bring us together again.
Please protect our home against the cold weather.
In Jesus' name I pray.
Amen.

A Love Note

Good Morning, My Darling.
I hope you enjoy your breakfast.
I love you, Honey!!!

My Prayer for You

Dear Father God,
Thank you for Your Grace & Mercy.
Lord there are so many things that we cannot understand, but we know
You are working every situation for our good.
Please keep us in perfect peace while we wait for our changes to come.
We trust in Your word that says, "They that wait on the Lord shall
renew their strength."
And Your word says that You will supply all our needs according to Your
riches in Glory.
Please keep Your arms around us and lead us in the path of
righteousness for Your name's sake.
We love you,
We trust in Your word,
We worship you, Lord.
Your children need you.
Please come now and see about us.
In Jesus Christ's name.
Amen.

Careful in the Cold

Good Morning, My Darling Husband.
Please be careful.
It's cold outside.

My Prayer for You

Father,
Father, I stretch my hands to You,
No other help I know.
I will lift my eyes unto the hills from which come my help.
All my help comes from the Lord, who made heaven and earth.
Father God, please forgive us for our sins and have mercy on us
according to Your lovingkindness.
Thank You for hearing and answering our prayers.
We plead the precious blood of Jesus over our lives.
We employ Your Holy Spirit to indwell us and keep us in all our ways.
Please protect us from evil.
Direct our footsteps.
Take control of our thoughts and tongue.
Help us to speak words of edification and not of destruction.
We praise You,
We worship You,
We love You for Who You Are.
In Jesus' Name
Amen.

When I'm Away

Good Morning, My Darling Husband.
I pray your day is blessed and safe.
I have to work late, but you will always be in my thoughts.
Enjoy your breakfast.

My Prayer for You

Dear Heavenly Father,
Thank you for Your grace and mercy.
Thank You for Your lovingkindness.
Please forgive us for our sins and create in us a clean heart and renew a right spirit in us.
Teach us Your ways and lead us in the path of righteousness for Your name's sake.
Thank You for opening Your storehouse of blessings on our marriage and families.
Keep Your arms around our children and grandchildren.
Protect them from all hurt, harm, and danger.
We have a mound of bills, Father.
Please show us a way out.
The earth is Your and the fullness thereof.
We trust in You and Your unfailing word.
In Jesus Christ's name we pray.
Amen.

Breakfast Blessings

Good Morning, My Love!!!
I didn't know what to fix for your breakfast.
I cooked for you and I hope you enjoy it.
I miss you, Honey.
Someday we will have more time together.
I'm going to cut Mondays out so we can spend more time together.
My prayer for us is that God helps us to hold out until our changes come.
They will come.
I love you!!!

My Prayer for You

Lord, please take care of us and keep us safe while we are apart and bring us together again.
Be with my husband as he leaves home and travels the streets to work.
Send Your angels to protect us.
In Jesus' name.
Amen.

I Want to Be Your Peace

My Dearest Husband,
I love you so much.
I have to admit I wish I could do something to bring more peace
to your mind.
I want you to know we will be alright.
I pray you get a full-time job, but until that happens, I want you
to not worry.
God is still in the blessing business and He has not forgotten us.
This is my prayer for us.

My Prayer for You

Dear Heavenly Father,
Thank You for our marriage and life together.
Thank You for keeping us safe and providing all our needs.
Lord, You know our problems
In Jesus Christ's name.
Amen.

I Am So Proud of You

Good morning, Darling...
I pray you are having a blessed day.
I am so proud of you for continuing to work on your book.
Please don't take a setback as a loss.
You will complete it and get it published soon.
I have faith in you and your ability.
This is my prayer for us....

My Prayer for Change

Dear Heavenly Father,
For Your goodness, mercy, grace, and love, we thank You.
For never leaving us and always keeping us, we thank You.
For protecting us and leading and guiding us, we thank You.
You created us in Your image and after Your likeness and for
that, we say thank You.
You told us that whatever we ask in Jesus' name, You would
grant us and we thank You for Your promises because Your word is
truth.
Lord, please bless my husband to be the man, father, and
husband You created him to be.
Please bless me to be the woman, mother, and wife You created
me to be.

Let our lives bring glory and honor to Your name.
Forgive us for our sins and cleanse us from all unrighteousness.
Let Your will be done in Earth as it is in Heaven.
In Jesus' name, we pray. Amen

I'm Only a Call Away

Good morning, my Darling Husband...
Babe, dress warm this morning and be careful.
God has His angels covering you.
Please call me when you get to work.
I promise the phone will be right by my ear.
I love you more than words can say.
My prayer for us...

My Prayer for You

Dear Heavenly Father,
Thank You for being a Fence around us on yesterday and keeping us safe.
Thank You for taking my husband to work and bringing home safe.
Even though the streets are covered with ice, Father, I trust You to protect him this morning as he drives in these conditions to and from work.
Lord, please drive for him and all the other people that has to be out.
Please go before him and make his path safe.
Thank You for hearing and answering our prayers.
We love and adore You.
Please accept our praise in Jesus' name.
Amen!

Please be Careful

Good morning, my Darling Husband,
Please be careful and watch out for black ice.
Please call me when you got to work.
I am praying all the way.

My Prayer for Protection

Lord God in Heaven,
Please protect my husband while he travel on the dangerous
streets.
Take control of the wheel and guide him safely to and from
work.
Please keep him healthy.
Bless his dreams and lead and guide him in the right path.
This I ask in Jesus' name.
Amen!

It's Going to Happen

Good morning, My Love.
You should be okay going in this morning, it's the drive back
that might be a little rough.
However, God has His angels keeping your safe.
I am so proud of you and look forward to you getting your book
published.
It's happening, Babe!
This is my prayer for us...

My Prayer for You

Dear Heavenly Father,
Thank You for the lady that is blessing my husband with the
publication of his book.
Thank You for the extra hours at work and thank You for
preparing him for the full time position You are preparing for him.
You are our Father and You said whatever we ask in Your Son
Jesus Christ's name shall be done.
Thank You for Your promises because all Your promises are Yea
and Amen.
So we thank You in advance, believing by faith we shall have
these things that we ask.

Your word said we are the head and not the tail.

We are the lender and not the borrower.

You said we are blessed when we go out and we are blessed when we come in.

We are blessed in the city, and we are blessed in the fields.

And our Father, we love and adore You and Your awesome love toward us.

Please protect my husband as he travels the dangerous highway and byways.

Keep us safe until we are together again.

Bless our children, grandchildren, and family.

Lord, give us a heart after Your own heart that we can love, live, and give like You.

Please forgive us for our sins and we forgive those who have sinned against us.

Thank You for our daily bread.

We pray this prayer in the Name that is above all names.

In the Name of Your Darling Son Jesus Christ, Who hung, bled and died for us.

Amen.

Short and Sweet

Good morning, Honey Baby!
Dress real warm today...it's cold out there.
Thank you for loving me.
This is my prayer for us today...

My Prayer for You

Dear Heavenly Father,
Thank You for being so good to us.
Thank You for providing all our needs.
You have protected us from all hurt, harm, and danger.
For that, we are so thankful.
You have given us a home to live in so we are not outside.
You have given us automobiles so we are not standing out in the cold.
You have given us food and clothes.
Lord, we are so thankful, but most of all, You have given us eternal life.
Our hearts rejoice in You, Lord.
Please watch over us while we are apart and bring us together again safe
and unharmed.
Thank you for the extra hours for my husband.
Give him patience to wait until You open the door of full-time
employment.
In Jesus' name.
Amen!

Please Watch Out...

Good morning, my Darling Husband!
Please be careful on your way to work.
A tree fell...
I love you and I pray you will be okay.
Please call me when you get to work.
This is my prayer for us today....

My Prayer for You

Dear Heavenly Father,
Thank You for taking care of us and keeping us safe.
I ask You to send your Holy Spirit and angels to protect all who must
drive on the dangerous streets tonight.
Please keep my husband from all hurt, harm, and danger.
Take the wheel and keep his truck on the road.
Lord, this is Your weather, and we are Your children.
I know You have not given us a spirit of fear.
Thank You for the bravery of my husband and for his determination to
take care of his family.
Please heal his body and take away the cold and fever.
Thank You, Father, for Your love, mercy, and grace.
Keep us safe until we are together again.
In Jesus Christ's name, I pray.
Amen!

St. Patrick's Day

Don't forget to wear something green today, it's St. Patrick's Day.
I know we have our moments, but I do really love you.
This is my prayer for us today....

My Prayer for You

Dear Heavenly Father,
Thank You for all Your many blessings You've bestowed on us.
Thank You for our marriage relationship.
Thank You for supplying all our needs and even giving us some of our wants.
Thank You for opening the door for my husband to get a full-time job.
Lord, please go before him and touch the hearts of those who can help him acquire the job.
We praise Your name for loving us.
Thank You for forgiving us of our sins.
Thank You for keeping us safe from all hurt, harm, and danger.
Keep Your angels encamped around about us day and night.
Protect my husband as he travels to work in the dark of night and watch over me as I sleep.
Keep the thieves and robbers away from our home.
Lord, we put all our trust in You.
Please bless our finances so we can get out of debt.

Please heal my husband from his cold.

We will forever give You the glory for all You have done, are doing, and will do.

In Jesus' name, we pray.

Amen!

I Appreciate You

You are my Priest, Protector, and my King.
I am the most blessed woman alive to have you as my husband.
I really do appreciate all that you do to make sure I'm happy and
taken care of.
Don't you ever think you are anything less!

Thanking God in Advance

Dear Heavenly Father,
You are God Almighty and there is nothing impossible for You.
Your word says we can do all things through Christ which
strengthens us.
Lord, we are in a dark place in our finances, jobs, and
relationship.
Please shine Your holy light on us and show us the way.
Open our eyes so that we can see Your work through these rough
times.
For we know that all things work together for good to those who
love You and are the called according to Your purpose.
Lord, we place all our faith and hope in You, knowing You will
always take care of Your own.
Thank You, Father, for hearing our prayers and keeping us from
the harm of this evil world.
Thank you for protecting us as we go to and from places.
Thank You for protecting our home.
Thank you for providing all our needs according to Your riches in
glory.

Lord, the earth and everything in it belongs to You.
There is nothing and no one that You do not have complete control of.
The people on my husband's job are coming against him.
Father, please turn the situation around for his good and forgive them for they do not know what they are doing.
Your word says it is better that they would tie a stone around their necks and drown in the sea than to hurt one of Your little ones.
Please have mercy on them.
Loose the bonds that's holding my husband up from full-time employment.
Bless our finances that every bill is paid in full.
Bless us that we can be a blessing to others.
Lord, we will forever give You the glory and praise for Your wonderful works in our lives.
In Jesus Christ's name, we pray.
Amen!

A Faith Prayer...

I declare and decree in the name of Jesus Christ by the power of the Holy Spirit that your throat is healed.

That your sinuses are clear.

That your blood pressure is normal.

That you will succeed in attaining the job of your dreams.

That you will be able to take care of your family the way you desire.

That your spirit life will be where you desire it to be.

That our marriage will be a happy union.

That no weapon formed against you will prosper.

That your enemies will not come near you.

That you are the man God created you to be.

That someday men will be coming to you for help because you will be waking in your destiny.

You are precious in the eyes of your Heavenly Father and there is nothing He will not do for you.

Lift up your head, husband, and look to the hill from where your help comes.

God is able to complete the work He started in you.

In Jesus Christ's name, I pray and receive it by faith.

Amen!

Looking Forward to You

Good morning, my Darling Husband!
I'm glad you feel better.
You are healed and everything is already working for your good.
I am looking forward to having you at home the next two nights.
I know you are working Saturday, but Saturday night, you are all mine!
I am so looking forward to your two-week vacation.
Try to save a little money to spend with your grandchildren and daughter.
I know the bills have to be paid, but it won't hurt to spend a little for family's sake.
God has heard our prayers and I believe He is answering as we continue to look unto the hills where our help comes.
All our help comes from the Lord Who made Heaven and Earth.

My Prayer for You

Thank You, Heavenly Father, for always taking good care of Your children.
You are a Father above all fathers.
You know our needs.
You are more than able to supply all our needs.
Your words tell us that no good thing would you withhold from us.

Thank you so much.
We praise Your name forever.
In Jesus Christ's name, we pray.
Amen!

Don't Worry About Me

Good morning, my Darling Husband!
I will be traveling today but try not to worry about me.
I have my angels encamped all around me.
You be careful and take good care of yourself because I'm coming
back, and I'll need a hug.

My Prayer for You

Dear Heavenly Father,
You have always been and always will be our Keeper and our
Protector.
Thank You for loving Your children so much that You will never
leave us or forsake us.
Today, my husband and I will be miles apart, but I know Your
presence will be with the both of us.
Please give him peace so he doesn't worry and see me safe to
Jackson and back.
Thank you for giving him extra hours while we wait patiently for
a full-time position that you are moving him toward.
Thank You for blessing our marriage, family, and finances.
Thank You for your healing power and for healing my husband.
The joy of the Lord is our strength.
You are our Refuge and our Strength.

We praise Your Holy Name.
We pray this prayer in Jesus Christ's name.
Amen!

I Enjoyed You

Good morning, Darling!
It's been a really good two weeks.
I have enjoyed having you home, especially at bedtime.
To have you close to me while we slept was the best part of my
day.
I will miss you.
But my prayers will always be with you.

My Prayer for You

Dear Heavenly Father,
I am grateful for the time you gave my husband and I to bond.
Thank You for a wonderful man and even greater friend.
Please watch over us while we are apart and protect us from all
hurt, harm, and danger.
Keep us in perfect peace until You open the door of full-time
employment for my husband and finances for our family.
Lord, you know what we stand in need of, and you know just
how to bless us.
Thank You for all Your benefits toward us.
In Jesus' name.
Amen!

A Few Words

Good morning, Honey!
I pray you had a good night's rest.

My Prayer for You

Dear Heavenly Father,
I come to You with thanksgiving in my heart for blessing me
with a wonderful husband.
One that loves You with all his heart and strives to do Your will.
One who loves me the way You commanded him to.
Thank You, Lord.
Thank You for Your lovingkindness towards us and providing us
with all our needs.
Thank You for protecting us from all hurt, harm, and danger.
Thank You for blessing our home, children, grandchildren,
Mother, and family.
Father, please accept our praise because You alone are worthy.
Thank You for opening doors for us to minister to your people.
Lead and guide us in the path of righteousness for Your name's
sake.
Lord, give us a heart to love the way You will have us to love.

Help us to be on one accord in mind and spirit.
Teach us to treat each other with respect and care.
Thank You, Father, for what You have done, are doing, and have
promised to do because Your promises are Yes and Amen!
In Jesus' name, I pray.
Amen!

My Prayer for You

Dear Heavenly Father,
Here we are again bowing before Your throne of grace and
mercy.
We come with grateful hearts for all Your many blessings.
Thank You for salvation.
Thank You for blessing our marriage, our finances, our home,
our children, grandchildren, Mom, and our family.
Father, You have been so good to us.
You have kept us safe and healthy.
You have forgiven all our sins.
We love you, Lord.
According to Your word we have not because we ask not.
This morning, we are asking for a special blessing.
Please give us a financial blessing.
Any way You choose is alright because all good and perfect gifts
come from You.
Thank You for keeping us safe from all hurt, harm, and danger.
Keep Your loving arms of protection around us as we travel to
and from work.
Watch over our home and protect us.
Lord, we put all our trust in You and Your provision because we
know You care for us.
We pray this prayer in Jesus' name.
Amen!

Breakfast Substitution

Good morning, my Darling!
I made you breakfast.
I hope grits are okay.
I noticed all the oatmeal was gone.
Enjoy!

My Sunshine

Good morning, my Darling!
You are my sunshine,
My only sunshine.
You make me happy
When skies are gray.
You'll never know, Dear,
How much I love you.
Please don't take
My sunshine away!

Thank you for such a good job cutting the yard.
It is beautiful!
I love you, my husband.

My Prayer for You

Dear Heavenly Father,

Thank You so much for all Your benefits toward us.

They are too many to name one by one, but we thank You for them all.

Please continue to keep us safe from all hurt, harm, and danger.

Place Your angels around our children, grandchildren, and family.

Bless Momma and keep her under the wings of Your love.

We love You and place all our trust in You.

Please bring my husband to the place of getting his book published.

Bless his writing.

Thank You in advance for his full-time job and blessing our finances.

We will forever praise Your name.

In Jesus' name, we pray.

Amen!

Thank You for Encouraging Me

Good morning, Honey.
I love you so much.
You are the apple of my eye.
My class went really well last night.
You were right about the teacher.
The way he starts his class is a little crazy, but he was really good tonight.
He doesn't remember your name, but he was at the Med when you were there.
Thank you for encouraging me to continue.

My Prayer for You

Lord,
Thank You for my husband.
Thank You for loving me enough to give me a wonderful husband to spend the rest of my life with.
Please keep him safe from all hurt, harm, and danger.
Watch over me while we are apart until we are together again.
Thank You for blessing our home and every area of our lives.
Please open the door of full-time employment for my husband.
Place him in the right place to advance him in his job.
We love you.
We honor you and praise your name.
In Jesus' name, we pray.
Amen!

Have a Good Day

Good morning, Love of my life.
I love you, Honey.
Pray you have a great day.
Hugs & Kisses

My Prayer for You

Dear Heavenly Father,
Thank You for all Your blessings You've showered on us.
Thank You for your grace and mercy and Your lovingkindness toward us.
Thank You for blessing our marriage, families, home, jobs, and every area of our lives.
Thank You for health and strength.
Please protect us and keep us from all hurt, harm, and danger.
Send your angels to encamp around us as we travel the dangerous highways.
Thank You for salvation.
Lord, You are our Strength and our Lord and Saviour and we are really grateful for all You do for us.
Thank You in advance for blessing my husband with a full-time position.

Please show him favor.
We will praise Your name all the days of our lives.
Thank You for hearing and answering our prayers.
In Jesus' name, we pray.
Amen!

Enjoying Our Time Together

Dear Husband,
I have really enjoyed our time together this week and looking
forward to another three-day weekend this week.
We are really blessed.
I pray you have a wonderful day.
I have choir rehearsal tonight.
I'll try to come home a little early today, but I can't promise.
Thank you for cutting the yard.
I love you, Honey.

My Prayer for You

Dear Heavenly Father,
Thank You for Your lovingkindness and Your tender mercies.
Thank You for protection, provision, and salvation.
You are still God and besides You there is none other.
Thank You for not only hearing our prayers but answering them.
Lord, we realize we don't deserve all Your kindness, but we thank you.
Please show my husband what to do to get his book published and
where to go to live his dream as a motivational speaker.
Lord, we place all our cares upon you because we realize without You we
can do nothing, but with You nothing is impossible.
We are living in expectation of what You are doing.
We give You all the glory, honor, and praise.
In Jesus name...
Amen!

Thank You for Loving Me

Good morning, my Darling Husband.
Thank you for loving me.
I really do appreciate you for all you do for our marriage and
home.
This is my prayer for us...

My Prayer for You

Dear Heavenly Father,
Thank You for all Your benefits toward us.
You have blessed us with a good life and health.
You are our Healer.
Please heal my husband's cold.
Give him strength and clear his head of congestion.
Bless him on the job.
Lord, let there be peace and harmony.
Please encamp Your angels around him and protect him from the
evil comments of the enemy.
Forgive the ones that pick on him and save them with Your
grace.
Thank You for the extra hours of work while we wait on the full-
time position.
Lord, lead him and guide him to the places and people to aid him
in moving forward.
Thank You, Lord, for giving us love for each other.
Lord, I have a special request.

Please bless our finances that we are able to pay our bills and not struggle next year.

We love You and we praise You.

We honor You and it is our desire to live for you.

In Jesus' name, I pray.

Amen!

Thank You for Choosing Me

Good morning, Honey!
It is such a blessing to have a wonderful, loving, and caring
husband.
You are truly a blessing from God.
Thank you for choosing me!

My Prayer for You

Dear Heavenly Father,
Holy is Your name, and the honor belongs to You.
You are our Creator, Keeper, and Redeemer.
Thank You for choosing us.
Thank You for hearing and answering our prayers.
You are our Provider, Protector, and High Priest.
All that we need, we find in You.
We love You with all our heart, mind, and strength.
We praise Your name forever.
Please encamp your angels around us and keep us from all hurt,
harm, and danger.
Shine Your light on our pathway so we can see You in all we do
or say.
Lead and guide us in the path of righteousness for Your name's
sake.
Give us peace in a world that ever seeks to pull us down.
You made us in Your image and after Your likeness.
We want to represent You well.
Be with my husband as he goes to and from work.

Let him have a peaceful day and good working conditions.
Thank you for healing his body and giving him the strength to support his family.
Thank You for giving him full-time employment with benefits.
Your word said ask and it shall be given, seek and you shall find, knock and the door shall be opened.
Thank You!
In Jesus' name, I pray.
Amen!

I Thank God for You

Dear Husband,
I thank God for you.
He gave you to me and all good and perfect gifts come from above.
You are good for me and you are the perfect husband for me.
Thank you, Honey, for your love and care you give to me.
You are a hardworking man and you are an awesome provider.
I pray that God blesses your every step.
My prayer for you is that God will enlarge your territory and keep all evil from you.
I pray that all your wishes and dreams come true.

My Prayer for You

Lord,
Please keep Your arms around my husband.
Keep him safe and give him peace.
Bless his health and be with him as he prepares for a new job.
We love and trust You, Father, and we thank You for all Your blessings.
In Jesus name, I pray.
Amen!

I'll Keep You in my Prayers

Good morning, Honey!
I love you.
I probably will not get a chance to see you today because I will not be getting get off until about 8:00 PM, but we will talk.
Keep me in your prayers as I am traveling.
I will keep you in mine.

My Prayer for You

Father in Heaven,
You have really been good to us.
Thank You for a good report from the doctor.
Now, Lord, we pray for strength to obey the dietary law and eat the right food that You have provided us.
Give us the wisdom to properly take care of our bodies because our bodies are Your temple.
Keep us from temptation and, if we are tempted, please keep us strong.
Watch over us today and keep us safe from harm.
Go with me as I travel and my husband while he goes to and from work.

Lord, bless our families, our home, our finances, our children, and Mom.
Thank You for Your grace and mercy.
In Jesus' name, I pray.
Amen!

I Missed You

Good morning, my Darling Husband!
I missed you on yesterday.
I am praying for your healing.
I pray you have a good day at work today.
I have to go to work early this morning and I have to go have
blood drawn at 2:00, so I will see you at about 3:00.
Thank you for being a wonderful husband and I love you more
each day.

My Prayer for You

Lord,
Please protect my husband as he travels to and from work and
keep me safe.
Thank You, Father God, for Your lovingkindness and tender
mercies.
I'm glad Your grace is all we need.
We put all our trust in You, Father.
We cast all our cares on You because You care for us.
We praise You for everything because we know You are working
everything out for our good.
In Jesus' name, I pray.
Amen!

I'm Trying my Best

Good morning, My Darling!
I may not be the best wife, but I am trying to give you my best.

My Prayer for You

Dear God in Heaven,
Thank You for Your grace and mercy.
Thank You for Your provision and protection.
Please forgive us for our sins.
Give us a heart that loves with a Godly love.
Help us to treat each other the way Your word teaches us to.
Please bless our finances that we are not the tail and that we are
the lenders and not the borrowers.
Bless our home that it is a home of peace and love and not
confusion.
Thank you, Father, for hearing and answering our prayers.
In Jesus Christ's name, we pray.
Amen!

I'm Not Upset

Good morning, my Darling Husband.

I love you with my whole heart.

Please have a good day.

I'm not upset with you.

I'm just praying for me that God will show me how to be the best wife possible for you.

I have a lot to learn, but there is one thing I know and that is I really do love the Lord and I really do love you!

I pray for a heart like Jesus.

Please forgive me for hurting you.

Just because I don't understand you doesn't mean that I don't love you.

I have to learn to keep my opinions to myself.

I pray for us and I need you to pray for me.

Another Cold Day

Good morning, my Darling Husband!
Please dress warm...it's cold out there.
My prayer for us this morning....

My Prayer for You

Dear Heavenly Father,
We humbly bow before Your mighty throne to thank You for Your
mercy, grace, and lovingkindness.
Thank You for forgiveness and salvation.
Thank You for Your Holy Spirit Who indwells us and keeps us.
Father, we plead the blood of Jesus over our marriage, family,
bodies, minds, finances, home, and jobs.
Please search us and know us.
If You find anything that's not like You, move it and make us
whole.
Please lead us in the path of righteousness for Your name's sake.
Lord, we place all our faith in You for everything.
You know our needs and desires.
We place them all in Your hand, knowing You will supply them
according to Your riches in glory.
Please send Your angels to encamp around us and keep us safe
from all hurt, harm, and danger.
Bless my husband to get his book published and get full-time
employment.
Please allow our marriage to grow in a loving way to honor You.

We love You and give You all the glory for the things You have done.

We pray in Jesus' name.

Amen!

Thank You

Good morning, my Darling!
Thank you for last evening.
I love being in your arms.
You make me happy.
I love you.
Have a good day, my Love.

My Prayer for You

Father God,
Thank You for Your lovingkindness.
Thank You for keeping us in perfect peace.
Please keep us from all hurt, harm, and danger.
Please bless our marriage, children, family, and home.
We love You and put all our trust in You.
We ask that You lead and guide us in the way You will have us to
go that our lives will bring glory and honor to Your name.
In Jesus' name, we pray.
Amen!

Thank You for Doing all You Can

Good morning, my Dear Husband!
I love you.
Thank you for doing all you can to make sure we are taken care
of.
Thank you for all the hard work you do.
I know it is not easy but you get up every morning and go to
work and, when you are home, you do all you can to make me
comfortable.
Thank you.
I know we don't always agree on things, but I always love you.
Please know that!
I love it when you assure me and say, "We going to be alright."
I love it when you know I'm not feeling well and you take good
care of me.
Thank you.
I love how you warm the bed so when I come to bed, I don't have
to come to a cold bed.
Thank you.
Honey, I love you with my whole heart.
Have a good day, Honey, and take good care of yourself because
you belong to me!

I'm So Glad for You

Good morning, my Darling Husband!
I missed you on last evening.
So glad you got good news on your book.
I have to go to Collierville this morning, but I should be home a little early, so we can spend some time together before I go to aerobics.
My prayer for you is...

My Prayer for You

Dear Heavenly Father,
Thank You for Your lovingkindness and your tender mercies.
Thank You for sending people in my husband's life to help him complete his book.
Thank You for lifting him to his highest potential.
Bless him on his job, in his ministry, and even as he goes out and comes in.
Lord, thank You for our marriage.
Please bless us to come together in our thoughts so we are not on different sides.
Make us one.
Send Your angels to watch over us and keep us from all hurt, harm, and danger.

Lord, we honor You.
We love you and we thank You for everything.
In Jesus' name....
Amen!

How Do I Love You?

Good morning, my Darling Husband.
How do I love you, let me count the ways.
Well, there is not a number large enough because each day I love
you more and more.
Dress warm, baby, it's cold out there.

My Prayer for You

Dear Heavenly Father,
You are Most Holy and All Wise.
Thank You for all Your blessings You have given us.
We love You with all our hearts.
We honor You with our lives.
Thank You for protecting us to and from all our destinations.
Thank You for allowing angels to encamp around about us.
Please keep my husband safe on his way to work each night.
Thank You for opening the door of full-time employment and
allowing him to get his work published.
Thank You for sending people in his life to accomplish his goals.
Thank You for blessing our marriage to be a loving and healthy
marriage.
Keep us while we are apart until we are together again.
This we ask in Jesus' name. Amen

Forgive the Distractions

Good morning, my Darling.
Please forgive me for all the distractions last night.
Can I please have a raincheck?
Please be safe on your way to work.

My Prayer for You

Dear Heavenly Father,
Thank You for loving us and taking care of all our needs.
Please send Your angels to encamp around my husband tonight
as he travels to and from work, and keep him safe from harm all
through the day.
Lord, give him peace where there is confusion, joy where there is
sadness.

Keep his eyes, ears, and heart so that everything he encounters today will only edify him so he can glorify Your name.

Thank You for opening the door to a full-time position and even if You don't, we know You are able.

Lord, we put all our trust in You and Your word.

Now, may the Lord watch between me and you, while we are absent one from another.

In Jesus' name, I pray and give thanks.

Amen!

Leave the Water On

Good morning, my Love!
Please leave the water dripping before you leave.
And please be careful.

My Prayer for You

Thank You for my husband.
Thank You for loving us and taking care of all our needs.
Please send Your angels to watch over us while we are apart and
bring us safely together again.
Please protect us from all harm and danger.
Thank You for blessing my husband with enough finances to
support his family.
Thank You for keeping him healthy and at peace.
We love and trust Your word.
In Jesus Christ's name, I pray.
Amen!

Only God

Good morning, my Darling!
Only God can open doors that no man can close,
And close doors that no man can open.
There is nothing impossible with God!

My Prayer for You

Our Father in Heaven,
Thank You for hearing and answering our prayers.
Thank You for blessing our marriage union.
Thank You for keeping ALL of Your promises.
You told us if we delight ourselves in You, You would give us the
desires of our hearts.
Lord, you know my husband desires a full-time position, but we
know You know what doors need to be opened.
Father, we trust You in every area of our lives.
We love You, Father, and as a child would ask a father for a
favor, we humbly ask you for Your favor.
Please keep my husband safe and free from harm until we meet
again.
Thank You, Father God.
In Jesus' name, we pray.
Amen!

Straight into Prayer

Good morning, Babe!
I love you

My Prayer for You

Father God,
I pray for peace in our marriage and continued respect for one
another.
Please keep Your loving arms around us today as we travel to and
from work.
Thank You for Your lovingkindness, Your tender mercies, and
Your grace.
Lord, I know You have all power in Your hand, and You are able
to do anything but fail.
Please show favor on my husband and bless him with full-time
employment.
I thank You in advance for your blessing because Your word said
whatever we ask in Jesus' name, it shall be done unto us.

We are standing on Your promises and on Your word for Your promises are all Yes and Amen!

Give us this day our daily bread and forgive us our sins.

"Now unto Him who is able to keep us from falling and present us faultless before the presence of his glory with exceeding joy, to the only wise God our saviour, be glory and majesty, dominion and power, both now and forever."

Amen!

Straight into Prayer 2

Good morning, my Love.
I pray your day is Blessed

My Prayer for You

Dear Heavenly Father,
Thank You for my husband.
Please teach me to be the wife he so deserves and give me the
wisdom to make his home a good place.
Lord, please help our marriage to be what You would have it to
be so that our marriage can honor You.
Thank You for opening the door of full-time employment for my
husband.
Father, we walk by faith and not by sight.
Bless our finances that we will be stable.
We put all our trust in Your word that You would supply all our
need.
Please keep us safe until we are together again.
In Jesus Christ's name, I pray.
Amen!

Straight into Prayer 3

Good morning, Darling!
Remember, you can do all things through
Christ who strengthens you

My Prayer for You

Thank you for Your lovingkindness, Your tender mercies, and
Your grace.
Thank You for being our Refuge and our Hiding Place.
You are our Keeper and You supply all our needs.
Thank You, Father God, for opening the door of full-time
employment for my husband and closing the door of part-time
employment..
Give him the strength and wisdom to know where to look and
guide his every thought that he will know it is Your doing and it is
marvelous in Your eyes.
Please watch over him and me while we are apart until we are
together again.
In Jesus' name...
Amen!

A Simple "I Love You"

Good Morning, my Darling Husband,
I Love you so much.

My Prayer for You

Lord,
Please watch over my husband today.
Go before him and make his pathway straight and smooth.
I thank You for opening the door of full-time employment for
him and granting him the desires of his heart.
In Jesus' name, I pray.
Amen!

Happy Again

Good morning, Darling.
Thank you for loving me.
You have made me happy again and for that I am so grateful.
Wrap up good and stay warm because you belong to me and I
want you to be safe and healthy.

My Prayer for You

Dear Heavenly Father,
Thank You for Your grace and mercy.
You have given us all that we need and You stand willing to keep
us until You come back.
Thank You for hearing and answering our prayers.
You are able to do all things and You told us all we have to do is
ask and have faith in you to bring it to pass.
Lord, please open the door of a full-time job for my husband.
Please give him peace while he waits on You, knowing You will
deliver us out of all our troubles.
In Jesus Christ's name, I pray and give thanks.
Amen!

A Prayer to Understand Him

Good morning, my Darling Husband!
I STILL LOVE YOU!

My Prayer for You

Dear Heavenly Father,
Please forgive me for getting upset with my husband.
You gave him to me, and all good and perfect gifts come from above.
Please teach me how to treat him properly.
I love him, but sometimes, it's hard to understand him.
Please help me to be better.
Thank You for blessing our marriage with Godly love for one another.
In Jesus Christ's name, I pray.
Amen!

Blessings and Favor

Good morning, my Love.
I pray your day is blessed in every area.
That God releases His favor upon you.
I pray strength and peace for you.
I pray that our marriage will be strong and loving.
God knows all about our struggles and he has promised to supply
all our needs according to His riches in glory.

My Prayer for You

Thank you, Father God, for Your lovingkindness, Your mercy,
and Your grace. Now may the Lord watch between me and you
while we are absent one from another.
In Jesus Christ's name, I pray.
Amen!

Blessings to Abound

Good morning, my Darling!
My prayer for you is that God will bless you in every area of your life.
That He will show you His favor on your job.

My Prayer for You

Thank You, Lord, for the extra hours, and keeping us until You open the doors of full-time employment.
Thank You for giving us a loving, kind, and respectful relationship in our marriage.
Help us to exemplify Your love toward one another.
We praise you, oh Lord, and we are grateful for Your grace and mercy toward us.
Please keep us safe while we are absent one from another.
In Jesus Christ's name, I pray.
Amen!

Heart Love

Good morning, Darling.
My heart loves you.

My Prayer for You

Most Holy and All Wise God,
We enter into Your gates with thanksgiving, and into Your courts
with praise.
We are grateful to You and we bless Your name.
Thank You for blessing us in every area of our lives, our health,
finances, spirit life, our marriage, our jobs, our families, and even
those blessings that are too numerous for us to number.
Our hearts overflow with love toward You.
Thank You for leading and guiding us in the path of
righteousness for Your name's sake.
Please keep Your loving arms of protection around us while we
are absent one from another and bringing us safely together again.
We pray this prayer of thanksgiving in Jesus Christ's name.
Amen!

My Sweetness

Good morning, my Darling Husband.
You are sweeter than the honey from a honeycomb to me,
and I love you for that.

My Prayer for You

Dear Heavenly Father,
Thank You for my husband and family.
Thank You for providing all our needs and even blessing us with
some of our wants.
Thank You for keeping us from all hurt, harm, and danger.
Please send Your angles to watch over my husband while he
travels to and from work during the early morning hours.
Thank You for the extra hours while we wait for full-time
employment.
You are great and greatly to be praised.
Now please watch between us while we are apart until we are
together again.
In Jesus Christ's name, I pray...
Amen!

You Support Me

Good morning, my Love.
Thank you for understanding and supporting me.
I love you and I am so blessed to have you in my life.

My Prayer for You

Dear Heavenly Father,
Thank You for all Your many blessings. You are always looking out for us. You have given us Your love in our hearts and allowed us to share our lives with one another.
Thank You for giving my husband more hours and blessing him with patience to wait on full-time employment.
Your word said if we ask anything in Jesus' name, You will do it for us and we asked for a full-time position for my husband and we thank You in advance for the full-time position.
Please keep us safe while we are apart and bringing us together again.
In Jesus' name...
Amen!

To God Be the Glory

Good morning, Darling.
To God be the glory for the things He has done!

My Prayer for You

Dear Heavenly Father,
Thank You for Your grace and mercy.
Thank You for blessing our marriage, our home, our health, our family, and our finances.
Thank You for hearing and answering our prayers.
Father, please keep Your loving arms around us and lead us in the path of righteousness for Your name's sake.
Take control of our thoughts and actions.
Please direct our path now and forever.
We praise Your name.
In Jesus' name, we pray.
Amen!

You Are my Blessing

Good morning, my Darling Husband.
God has blessed me with a man of great integrity and strength.
I love you, my husband.
You are so thoughtful and considerate.
You are kind and loving.
You are such a hard worker and provider and protector.
I could never ask for a more loving and supportive husband and I
thank You from the bottom of my heart.

My Prayer for You

Thank You, Father God, for being our Guide and our Keeper.
We love and adore You.
Please keep my husband and me safe until we are together again.
In Jesus' name....
Amen!

Breakfast Buffet with a Side of Prayers

Good morning, my love.
Breakfast for my King:
Cheese grits
Scrambled eggs
Turkey burger
Coffee

I cooked two burgers in case you want to take a sandwich to work.
Enjoy, my darling, and have a blessed day.

My Prayer for You

Father God,
We thank You for Your lovingkindness and tender mercies.
We place our lives in Your hands.
In Jesus' name, we pray.
Amen!

Blessings before Church

Good morning, Honey.
I missed you yesterday.
I hope I get to see you today before VBS.
This is my prayer for us....

My Prayer for You

Dear Heavenly Father,
They say absence makes the heart grow fonder.
Please let that be true because my husband and I are so busy
these days and I miss him.
Thank You for keeping us safe from harm.
Thank You for blessing us and our families.
Thank You for our children and grandchildren.
Thank You so much for Mommy.
Bless her with Your best blessings.
Father, thank you for blessing our home, jobs, health, spirits,
finances, and everything You have given us.
Help us to have a life that is pleasing to You.
We love You and are grateful for all You have done, are doing,
and all that You promised to do.

Please protect us while we are absent from one another and
bring us together again.
We praise You, we love You, and we adore You.
In Jesus' name, I pray.
Amen!

I'm All Yours

Good morning, my Love.
VBS is over...
I'm all yours now, Baby!
Thank you for your love and patience.
I love you.
I brought your favorite food tonight.
Can't wait to hold you in my arms.

My Prayer for You

Dear Heavenly Father,
Thank You for seeing us through this week.
Thank You for the one that gave her life to you during VBS.
God, You are so good.
Thank You for the hours You are giving my husband while we wait for a full-time position.
Thank You for keeping us safe from hurt, harm, and danger.
Father, please comfort the families of those who lost loves one in senseless killings.
Lord, please have mercy on the one who committed the act.
Thank You for food, shelter, and clothing.
You have blessed us with all our needs, and we are grateful for Your lovingkindness.
Lord, make us better, forgive our sins, and cleanse us from all unrighteousness.
We praise Your name.
In Jesus' name, we pray.
Amen!

Another Short and Sweet

Good morning, Honey.
I love you.
I pray you have a good day.

My Prayer for You

Dear Heavenly Father,
Lord, I thank you for all Your love You've shown us and all the
ways You've kept us.
Lord, you know this world is in a bad way.
Please keep my husband safe on his way to work and while he is
traveling to and from his many destinations.
Please keep Your angels encamped around him.
Watch over me when he must leave me in the middle of the
night.
Lord, I put our lives in Your hands.
Thank You for giving my husband extra hours at work while you
prepare him for his full-time position that You have for him.
Keep him in perfect peace.
Show him what to do and lead him to the places he needs to be.
Lord, please bless our marriage, our children, our families.
Give us strength to hold on until our changes come.
In Jesus' name, I pray.
Amen!

My Heartbeat

Good morning, my Heartbeat.
I cooked, but it was too hot to put up.
I will do it when I get up.
Help yourself.
I pray you have a good safe day, Honey.

My Prayer for You

Dear Heavenly Father,
Holy is Your name.
Your kingdom come.
Your will be done in earth as it is in heaven.
Give us this day our daily bread.
Forgive us our debts as we forgive our debtors.
Lead us not inro temptation but deliver us from evil.
For Yours is the kingdom, power, and glory forever and ever.
Amen!

Please Rest

Good morning, Darling.
Hope you get some rest.
You are the apple of my eye.
I love you, Honey.

My Prayer for You

Dear Heavenly Father,
Thank You for Your lovingkindness, Your amazing grace, and Your mercy.
Thank You for blessing our marriage to be happy and healthy.
Thank you for providing for us through our jobs.
Thank You for opening door for us to give us a better life.
Thank You for Momma, our children, grandchildren, and our family.
Lord, please protect my husband as he travels the dangerous streets to and from work.
Please protect me and watch over us and bring us together again.
Lord, lead and guide us in the path of righteousness for Your name's sake.
We love You and place all our trust in You.
Teach us how to live the way you would have us to live.

Bless Your church to do the work You have prescribed and tell a
dying world that You are our Saviour.

We love You, Lord.

In Jesus' name, we pray.

Amen!

It's Been a While...

Good morning, my Darling.
I know it's been a while since I met you at the breakfast table,
but there was never a night I went to bed without praying for you.
I love you so much.
I'm sorry we are so busy.
It seems we hardly have time for each other.
So we are going to have to start trying to make more you and me
time.
I have no idea where to start, but we will do it together and soon.
I have faith in God because He is on our side.

My Prayer for You

Dear Heavenly Father,
Thank You for always taking care of us.
You have opened so many doors for us.
We need You to show us which one to enter and please guide us
through.
Lord, we need You to keep Your hands on us and keep us
grounded in You.
Let us not take anything for granted.
We realize that it's Your grace and mercy that have gotten us
this far and will lead us on.
We are so grateful for all You have given us, are giving us, and
will give us.

Thank You for extra hours on my husband's job, for the part-time job, and his writing.

We give You all the glory because it's all Your blessings.

Please watch over us as we travel the dangerous streets and keep us safe.

In Jesus' name....

Amen!

I'm Glad...

Good morning, my Darling.
I am glad you feel better.
I love you.

My Prayer for You

Dear Heavenly Father,
Thank You for answering prayer.
Lord, I praise Your name for Your lovingkindness, Your tender
mercy, and Your grace.
You allowed our friend and his family to make it home safe and
you gave my husband relief from his cold.
You are mighty, God and Father.
Thank You for blessing our children and grandchildren.
Lord, You have brought us almost through this year and we are
excited to see what You have in store for us in the next year.
Please keep us safe from harm and watch over us as we travel to
and from on the dangerous streets.
Father, thank You for keeping my husband from being robbed
and killed.
Please keep Your angels around him, protect him.
Father, I ask for peace on his job.
Remove all the negative people away from his area.
Keep him under Your wings of love and give him the strength to
keep his mind on You.

Lord, we love You and we are truly grateful to You for all Your
blessings.
In Jesus Christ's name...
Amen!

Thank You for Loving Me

Good morning, Honey.
I love you.
I pray you have a wonderful, blessed day!
Thank you for loving me.

My Prayer for You

Dear Heavenly Father,
Holy is Your name, and we thank You for Your mercy, grace, and lovingkindness.
Forgive us our debts as we forgive those who are indebted to us.
Give us this day our daily bread.
Lead us not into temptation but deliver us from evil.
Lord, the weather is predicted to be rough today.
Father, please keep my husband safe to and from work.
Keep Your angels around him and please take the wheel and drive the car.
Lord, heal his illness and comfort him.
Take away the pain and give him your peace.
Lord, bless our marriage that we become the married family You designed.
Give us the wisdom, patience, and understanding to love each other the way You intended us to.

Bless our home, families, children, finances, and every area of our lives.
We put all our trust in You because You are our Keeper and you love us with an everlasting love.
In Jesus' name, we pray.
Amen!

Praying for Your Health

Good morning, Honey.
I love you!
I hope you feel better today.
This is my prayer for us....

My Prayer for You

Dear Heavenly Father,
Thank You for Your grace and mercy.
Thank You for Your lovingkindness.
For keeping us from hurt, harm, and danger.
Thank You for our marriage and for allowing us to become better communicators.
Lord, You have allowed us to grow closer together and closer to You.
Thank you for the extra hours on my husband's job.
Lord, we still trust You for a full-time position. Your word said ask and we shall receive. We trust Your word.
Thank You for blessing our home, our children, and family.
Lord, please heal our bodies from the cold we are now battling.
Give us strength to make it through the holidays.
Bless every gift that will be given and received. Give safe travels to the ones traveling.

Thank You for Jesus Christ.
This I pray in Jesus' name.
Amen!

I'm a Happy Wife

Good morning, my Darling Husband.
I pray you have a wonderful day!
I love you, Honey, and I'm a happy wife.

My Prayer for You

Dear Heavenly Father,
Thank You for my wonderful loving husband.
Please heal his body of all illness and give him peace at work and
at home.
Bless him as he goes out and when he comes in.
Bless him on his job and in his ministry and enlarge his
territory.
Allow everything he sets his heart to do be blessed.
Lead and guide his steps and thoughts.
Please show him favor.
Bless our finances that we be able to pay our bills and not have
to fear no man.
Lord, we put all our trust in you and your plan for our lives.
Lord, we love You and are grateful for all Your blessings.
In the name of Jesus Christ, your Only Son, we pray.
Amen!

A New Year's Blessing

Good morning, Honey.
I love you so much.
I hope you have a good day.
I am really looking forward to sharing Christ with you at
midnight.
There is only one I would love to spend the old year out and new
year in with—that's you.

My Prayer for You

Our Father, which art in Heaven,
Holy is Your name.
Your kingdom come,
Your will be done, in earth as it is in heaven.
Give us this day our daily bread and forgive us out debts as we
forgive our debtors.
And lead us not into temptation but deliver us from evil.
For thine is the kingdom, power, and glory forever.
Amen!

Straight into Prayer 4

Good morning, Honey.
I love you.
This is my prayer for you today.

My Prayer for You

Dear Heavenly Father,
Thou Who was and is, and is to come.
The First, and the Last.
The Great I Am.
The Maker and Creator of all things.
Our Rock and our Shield.
Our Peace and Joy.
Lord, I have special request.
Please hear my prayer.
I ask you to bless my husband with a special blessing.
Give him a peace of mind.
Bless him to be the man, husband, and father You created him to be.
Increase his faith and open the door of success he needs to hold his head up high and show forth Your glory.
I know there is nothing impossible with You and You live in us, therefore all things are possible to us through Jesus Christ.
You know what he needs and just how to place him in the right position for him to be the provider, protector of his family.

Lord, I love You and I thank You in advance for Your grace and mercy.

In Jesus' name...

Amen!

About the Author

Queen E. Gardner was born January 26, 1953 in Batesville, Mississippi and moved to Memphis, Tennessee at age eleven. Her father died when she was eight years old.

She is the youngest child of sixteen children and was blessed to have many women in her life to direct her on life's journey. Her mother, a devout Christian and the mother of twelve daughters and four sons, was the biggest influence in her life. She taught her to always pray about everything and believe that her prayers were heard and answered by God. Her faith has always been the center of her life. She loves sharing her faith with everyone she meets.

She is a 1970 graduate of Douglass High School and Memphis School of Commerce where she got her degree in Executive Secretarial work, but quickly decided this was not her lifelong dream and went into management.

She is a renown soloist who has many rendered concerts for various occasions. In 2002, she was called into the preaching ministry and, in 2017, she was ordained in the Baptist Church. She has served in many teaching ministries and has spoken at events nationwide.

After 28 years of service, she retired from Tennessee State University Cooperative Extension Service where she served as a 4-H Program Assistant.

She is married to Courtney Gardner and is the mother of four children, two daughters and two sons, and the stepmother of one daughter.

She loves music, spiritual counseling and caring for people everywhere. Her dream is to someday learn to play the piano so she can be her own musician.

Her favorite quote: *"If a man is called to be a street sweeper, he should sweep streets even as Michelangelo painted, or Beethoven composed music or Shakespeare wrote poetry. He should sweep streets so well that all the hosts of heaven and earth will pause to say, 'Here lived a great street sweeper who did his job well."* ~ Dr. Martin Luther King Jr.

Daily Prayer:

Printed in Great Britain
by Amazon